Accession no.
00984146

Staff and Educational Development Association

Key Skills in Higher Education: Background and Rationale

Sue Drew
Sheffield Hallam University

SEDA Special No. 6
March 1998
ISBN 0 946815 89 5

Contents

Introduction

Over recent years there has been an increasing interest in Higher Education, and in education generally, in the development of generic attributes which have been termed transferable skills, personal skills, core or key skills. There has been a range of initiatives arising from this interest. The upsurge in activity raises a number of questions: what is the basis for these initiatives; where do they come from and how are they justified; what are the skills initiatives and what does the terminology mean?

It is also linked to fundamental questions about the nature of education. What are the purposes of education? Do educational establishments exist to preserve and advance knowledge, to produce cultivated individuals, to prepare people for life and/or work, or for a mixture of these, or indeed other, aims? Is education for the good of students, academics, the community, employers, the nation, or for any or all of these groups?

There is a particular view of education which links the economic success of the nation to educational establishments' ability to develop individuals who can cope with life in general and work in particular. In reviewing the arguments in favour of this view and their logical extension in the form of educational initiatives, this paper will consider four main areas:

* the development of the debate about the purposes of education
* what is meant by terms such as transferable skills, core/key skills, capability, competence
* some of the contradictions in the justifications for skills approaches and dissent from the justifications
* relevant initiatives.

1 The Debate: What is Education For?

This section reviews the debate about the purposes of education which is linked to the upsurge in interest in skills, and reviews the political and economic justifications which are part of that debate.

1.1 The educational context of the debate

The Great Debate about the purposes of education was set in train by James Callaghan in 1976. The context for this debate was the tradition of liberal education in this country, and an economy in increasing difficulties.

Schools and liberal education

Schools in this country, according to the Spens Report of 1938, had their roots in vocationalism. Spens claimed that the Grammar Schools which provided the model for our secondary education were originally linked to university education, which from medieval times had been largely vocational, though by the sixteenth and seventeenth centuries few pupils actually went to university and some were bound to trades.

By the eighteenth and nineteenth centuries the Public Schools began to emphasise the classics, developing the concept of "liberal education", their prestige being such that other schools followed their lead. Whilst liberal education could be viewed as a preparation for elite careers in administration or government, it was not vocationally relevant to the majority of secondary school pupils. Although there were attempts to make the curriculum more 'relevant', these usually foundered. Spens blames the value attached to Public School liberal education for the prejudice against vocational and technical education, and, to some extent, for the uniformity of our school education. Spens' attribution of such power to the liberal education tradition seems justified by the failure of his report to lead to the establishment of technical high schools.

In the 1960s the secondary school system was still largely based upon the grammar school model, geared to those who would go to university to study a specific subject, although the majority never reached this end point but dropped out along the way.

Higher Education and liberal education

Medieval universities prepared students for specific vocations such as the Church, law and medicine. In the nineteenth century universities were influenced by their German counterparts and the norm became to study one subject in depth (Burgess 1977). Burgess feels this focus on individual disciplines led to the discipline being self-justified rather than justified in terms of its usefulness, to a concentration in universities on research rather than teaching, and to a lack of interest in professional and vocational education.

Newman (1853) saw university education as developing a range of attributes in the individual which were independent of the subject studied

> *"to see things as they are, to go right to the point, to disentangle a strain of thought, to detect what is sophistical, and to discard what is irrelevant..."* The university graduate was able to *"accommodate himself (sic) to others"*, was *"at home in any society"*, knew *"when to speak and when to be silent"* and enjoyed *"the repose of a mind that lives in itself while it lives in the world (Newman 1853, p135).*

1.2 The development of the debate

The purposes of HE

"The Great Debate" had its beginnings in the 1960s, when both schools and universities placed value upon a liberal education unrelated in the main to vocational needs. The Robbins Report of 1963 recommended the establishment of Polytechnics, leading to a major expansion of Higher Education. Robbins saw the aims of education as being to develop employment-related skills, to produce cultivated people, to search for truth, and to transmit a common culture and standards of citizenship. In 1965, Anthony Crossland in his Woolwich speech advocated that a substantial part of HE should respond directly to social needs (Burgess and Pratt 1974), and the Swann Report (Committee on Manpower Resources for Science and Technology 1968) referred to the mismatch between graduate output and employment.

Atkins (1995) suggests there are currently four purposes of Higher Education: to provide a general educational experience of intrinsic worth; to prepare students for knowledge creation, application and dissemination; to prepare students for specific professions or occupations; to prepare students for general employment. In his report on Higher Education (NCIHE 1997), Dearing sees four main aims for HE: the development of the individual and personally so that they can grow intellectually, be equipped for work and contribute to society; to increase knowledge and encourage its application; to serve the needs of the economy; to contribute to a democratic, civilised, inclusive society. All have employment as a focus.

The debate and skills approaches

There are three main themes behind the political and economic justifications for skills approaches:

- rapid social and technological change
- the need because of such change for individuals to be highly skilled and to be able to transfer those skills to new situations
- the relationship between individuals' abilities and the nation's economic performance.

Rapid change

During the 1960s Britain's empire disappeared, our economy was in difficulty, and by the 1970s economic problems had led to increasing unemployment. By the early 1980s it was clear that this unemployment was not temporary but was related to long term changes in the structure of industry and employment.

In 1972 the Faure report for UNESCO on world-wide education referred to a rapidly changing world for which many existing education systems were no longer appropriate, concluding that:

- education designed for a minority when knowledge changed slowly was inappropriate for mass education when knowledge, influenced by advancing technology, changes rapidly
- traditional academic disciplines were valued disproportionately to their current usefulness.

Faure described education as under fire world wide for irrelevance to contemporary needs at a time when education was second only to defence in the world's national budgets. Education should equip people to cope with change.

Rapid change in knowledge, technology and society results in a need for adaptable people who will continue to learn throughout life - this became a major theme in the justifications for skills approaches. Knowledge may become outdated, but the skills needed to acquire and use new knowledge will not.

The need for skills

In 1976 Jim Callaghan opened "The Great Debate" in earnest, stating in his Ruskin Speech:

> *"The goals of our education, from nursery through to adult education are clear enough. They are to equip children to the best of their ability for a lively constructive place in society and also to do a job of work....There is no virtue in producing socially and well adjusted members of society who are unemployed because they do not have the skills." (Callaghan 1976)*

This was to become a major theme in the justifications for skills approaches to education throughout the 1970s and 80s - the need in an advanced technological society for a highly skilled workforce. The growing unemployment of unskilled people through the 70s and 80s gave an urgency to this theme. From 1980 there appeared a barrage of materials, government sponsored and otherwise, in which the importance of linking education to employment and of developing 'transferable personal skills' predominates. The proliferation of these materials coincided with the realisation that unemployment was a permanent problem, and with new attitudes of the Conservative governments towards economic regeneration.

These materials supported an argument which can be simply expressed as:

- Britain is in decline economically
- change in society and technology is now rapid
- in order to compete effectively and improve our economic performance we need people who are skilled and can transfer those skills to new situations
- the educational system must provide these people.

Skills and economic performance

In the 1980s Government thinking was influenced by a report on the vocational education and training (VET) policies of Japan, West Germany and the USA - "Competence and Competition" (MSC NEDO 1984), which made connections between economic success and the supply of skilled people, "skill" being used here in the sense of job related requirements. By the 1985 Green Paper "The Development of HE into the 1990s" (DES) very clear statements were being made about the key role of *"able, skilled and well motivated"* graduates in the country's economic success. The White Paper "Working Together - Education and Training (DoE/DES 1986), claimed

> *"The same machines are available to all. Success will go to those .... whose people can use them to the best advantage...People with their knowledge, learning, skills, intelligence, innovation and competence are our most important asset and resource" (DES 1986 p1)*

This view was reinforced by the Confederation of British Industry (CBI)

> *"To maintain and improve Britain's performance in an increasingly competitive world nothing short of a skills revolution is needed." (CBI 1990 p9)*

The assumption that links educating for skills and qualities with economic performance is now virtually unchallenged.

> *"The UK faces a world of increasing change; of ever fiercer global competition; of growing consumer power; and a world in which our wealth is more and more dependent on the knowledge, skills and motivation of our people." (DTI 1994)*

The Department of Trade and Industry (1994) describes a world in which barriers to the movement of goods and capital are falling, advances in technology have created new markets and transformed existing ones, population structures are changing with more older people and more women at work, and business is internationalised. It mentions a major UK company which handles customer relations in the UK and does its data processing in India. In 1991 there were 900,000 more small firms than in 1979. World trade is growing faster in services than in goods.

> *"In future, the most successful nations will be those which develop high quality, skilled and motivated workforces and make good use of them" (DTI 1994 p18).*

An Employment Department, Scottish Office, Welsh Office paper (1992) refers to an increasing *"emphasis on the role and importance of the individual employee" (p7),* and to the growth in the service sector and in white collar jobs - by 1990 32% of the workforce were in management or professional jobs. The UK is one of three EC countries where part-time workers amount to more than 20% of the workforce (part-time work increased in the UK by 34% between 1983 - 1990). Working patterns are more flexible, for example with annual contracts for specified hours, and there is a tendency away from collective agreements and towards individualism, with Trades Union membership falling.

The 1994 DTI document quotes National Targets for education and training in England and Wales, launched by the CBI and endorsed by the Conservative Government. These state that, for example, by 1997 80% of young people will reach National Vocational Qualification (NVQ) 2 or equivalent, and that education and training provision should develop self-reliance, flexibility and breadth.

A 1995 follow-up DTI paper reinforces the need for a highly skilled workforce and focuses on the need for individuals to *"take increasing responsibility for their own adaptability and reskilling" (p71).* It describes new National Targets which refer to core skills *"which will be developed through life"*.

> *"Through learning methods which encourage initiative and autonomy young people can develop their core skills within the National Curriculum and through the qualifications available to them at 16 and beyond. They can improve their core skills and make them more transferable through a range of opportunities to apply these skills in work-related settings, for example through managed work-experience and vocational options such as GNVQs and Modern Apprenticeships" (DTI 1995 p81).*

What sort of skills?

In 1980 the Finniston report referred to Britain's decline as a manufacturing nation, and to the low status attached to engineering. This low status reflected the value given to 'liberal education' and the dichotomy between education and training. Finniston was also concerned about our resistance to change and the level of skills in our engineers:

" ... almost the only factor that distinguished firms using a new technique from those not doing so was the existence in the 'innovative' firm of one or two key individuals who had the necessary expertise" (Finniston 1980 p38)

"Our discussions with employers revealed that the shortages they perceived were sometimes concerned with the experience and personal qualities they sought rather than with absolute numbers of engineers." (Finniston 1980 p54)

The Department of Employment gave further weight to these arguments in their New Training Initiative Consultative Document (MSC 1981). Jobs requiring limited skills were disappearing, 600,000 having been lost between 1971 and 1978, and it was predicted that white collar jobs would outnumber blue collar ones by 1985.

As the 1980s progressed it became clear that demography and global competitive forces would affect the demand for a skilled adaptable workforce, and that 'new' sources of labour would be needed - women, ethnic minorities, the unemployed, and older people (Department of Employment 1988).

Anderson and Marshall (1996) summarise the changes in employment structures and practices as follows:

1970s   bureaucratic, prescribed tasks

1980s   focus on business operations, more people responsible for quality and management of situations

1990s   empowerment, flatter, slimmer organisations, more people responsible for managing part of the business

They describe employment in the 1990s as having cross-functional structures, multi-discipline team working, increased delegation, and a greater concern with quality. Competition is intensified and internationalised, information technology (IT) has spread and employer structures must allow them to adapt quickly to changing circumstances. Technology means that fewer routine tasks are done by people, who are now needed for non-routine tasks. Anderson and Marshall refer to the decline of occupation specificity and refer to

".... the cross-occupational mixes of skills, which are now commonplace. The concept of occupation-specific (as opposed to job specific) is an anachronism" (1996 p23).

Different skills were needed in individuals for the differing employment structures of the 70s, 80s and 90s, according to Anderson and Marshall. In the 1970s basic skills such as reading, writing and numeracy were required, together with openness, honesty and reliability. In the 1980s occupation specific skills and knowledge were required, as were personal competences such as assertiveness. In the 1990s overarching capabilities became more important. Flatter organisations and greater delegation of responsibility meant employees need to be more motivated, more autonomous, have more initiative, be more capable of business thinking and more oriented towards outcomes. Core skills are not seen as more important than technical skills but there is

*"a growing emphasis on generic skills **with** occupation or job-specific skills ...." (p32)*

Anderson and Marshall quote evidence to indicate not only that employers perceive a skills gap in their recruits, but also that they tend to use selection tests to avoid employing people who need remedial training.

"Employers selection processes are aimed at excluding those not possessing the personal characteristics which are considered essential" (p 34)

Binks (1996) indicates that large firms are reducing their graduate recruitment and are more selective. The public sector is unlikely to expand and small and medium sized employers (SMEs) are the most likely source of jobs. SMEs have less need

"for high level knowledge, relying more on employee flexibility, initiative, problem solving, independent learning and other qualities" (Binks 1996 p27).

The norm is no longer for graduates to enter a large employer's graduate training programme - they must rather be "ready to go" when they begin work. Large firms are seeking ways of reducing their core functions and often contract work out to SMEs, and flexibility is increasingly a requirement of employees.

Harvey et al (1997) interviewed a total of 258 respondents, strategic managers, line managers, and graduate and non graduate employees from 91 organisations, finding that graduate employment now includes a much wider range of jobs. There is less time for employees to 'get up to speed' in *"delayered, downsized, information technology driven, innovative organisations"* (Harvey et al 1997 p1). Adaptive graduates are essential. These are people who can fit in quickly, tend not to take risks, do the job required and avoid questioning established procedures, which they adapt according to circumstance. However, employers also need 'transformative employees', people who will transform and change the organisation.

"Transformative attributes tend to include such things as critique, synthesis, and enabling leadership. Transformative agents by definition have ideas, 'look outside the box', cause friction and look ahead" (Harvey et al 1997 p23)

Adaptive and transformative attributes are part of a continuum.

"...the difference between adding value and transforming....is about the way a range of skills and abilities are applied. It is the difference between fitting into a team, working in a team, and getting the team to push the boundaries" (Harvey et al 1997 p24)

Harvey's respondents listing of the attributes required included intellect, self regulatory skills such as self motivation, interactive skills such as written communication, oral communication (the most frequently mentioned 'transferable skill' in job advertisements) and IT, and teamwork and interpersonal skills. Teamwork, communication and teamwork are inextricably linked in the 'delayered' organisation - all contribute to 'fitting-in', persuading, developing ideas and transforming.

1.3 The debate and Higher Education

The Great Debate is set, then, within the context of increasing concern about the nation's economy and an increasing focus on the contribution the individual makes to that economy. Graduate unemployment in the 1970s led to a questioning of the appropriateness of HE for today's world, and changes in the composition of the student body and Government concerns about value for money have all added to pressures to review teaching and learning in HE.

Undergraduate education and the job market

While graduate employment remained buoyant in the 1960s there was little questioning of the premise that HE places should be provided according to choice, and universities had a vested interest in a system which was based largely on the intellectual interests of students and academics (Williams 1985). It was assumed that graduates would find work to suit themselves and the economy (Boys et al 1988).

In the 1970s the graduate unemployment rate rose because of slower economic growth and lower public spending. Graduate unemployment had a significant effect upon the values attached to discipline areas and influenced views of the purposes of HE and of the preparedness of students for life after graduation. Boys and his colleagues' 1984-7 study into how undergraduate teaching responded to the labour market, found that while in the early 1980s the view was still prevalent that traditional academic values would lead to graduates being well-suited to the labour market, by 1987 this had changed. Governments from 1980 had little sympathy with the notion that undergraduates can develop economically useful abilities without deliberate attention to these skills by HE courses.

During the 1980s the graduate employment situation improved. The Central Services Unit of The Association Of Graduate Careers Advisory Services (CSU 1990) estimated a 2.5% increase in the numbers of graduates for 1990 over 1989 and an increase of 3% in graduate vacancies. The resulting competition between employers' to recruit good graduates added a new dimension to the debate about education, and fuelled employers demands for what they perceive are the 'right sort' of graduates.

Harvey et al (1997) quote the Institute of Employment Studies as indicating that recruiters expected an increase of 18% in the number of graduate vacancies in 1995 over 1994, and that graduate unemployment was falling. Graduate opportunities are expanding, but outside the traditional graduate careers, a quarter of all graduates are employed by organisations with fewer than 25 employees, and there is a blurring of graduate and non graduate jobs. Harvey's survey suggested that it is hard to now obtain a management job without a degree. SMEs form an increasing part of the employment structures of the country and this has led to a wider range of graduate jobs. Additionally the increased number of graduates has led to employers considering them for traditionally non-graduate jobs, which in turn led to those jobs changing as employees have found graduates able to contribute more to them.

Teaching and learning in HE

In 1963 Robbins had begun to address issues related to Higher Education teaching and learning, suggesting that more weight be attached to staff's ability to teach than to research and that the lecture was limited as a means of instruction.

The Council for National Academic Awards (CNAA) had from its inception in 1964 included within "Principle 3" of its statutes a commitment to the personal development of students:

".... the development of students' intellectual and imaginative powers, their understanding and judgement, their problem solving skills, their ability to communicate, their ability to see relationships within what they have learned and to perceive their field of study in a broader prospective. Each student's programme of study must stimulate an enquiring, analytical and creative approach, encouraging independent judgement and critical self-awareness." (CNAA 1989 p18)

The 1985 green paper "The Development of Higher Education into the 1990s" (DES) indicated not only the Government's view of the importance of HE in providing suitably skilled people to aid the economy, but dissatisfaction with how well this task was being performed. The paper advocated the fostering of positive attitudes to industry, commerce, entrepreneurship and work, and of team work and leadership skills in graduates. HE it claimed, did not respond quickly enough to the economy, or always provide value for money.

Changes in the student body

The Debate has been influenced by the changing nature of the student body. Demographic downturns have meant both that education has vested interests in attracting non-traditional students and that Government has similar interests in better use of women, mature people and ethnic minorities in employment (although, CSU has noted no significant shifts in employer attitudes to mature graduates, nor much evidence of flexible working patterns or child care facilities which make work easier for women - CSU 1992. Harvey et al -1997- found that 'fast track' graduate recruiters tend to set an upper age limit of 25-30.). Since Robbins the imbalance between men and women in HE has slowly been redressed, though not uniformly between courses. As the 1980s progressed into the 1990s more mature students have entered education, particularly the former Polytechnics. There was a massive expansion in student numbers throughout the 1980s. In 1979 1 in 8 school leavers entered HE but by 1993 it was 1 in 3. The UK has the highest graduation rate in Europe (DTI 1994).

Value for money

The Conservative Governments in the 1980s became increasingly concerned about the return to the economy on the investment in education, a view shared by the CBI.

> *"The CBI believes that too few people take existing courses with adequate regard to their practical application...We believe there is a strong case for taking employment considerations into greater account in planning the development of higher and advanced further education (Education, Science and Arts Committee 1980 p 329, 330)*

The first planning exercise by the National Advisory Body (NAB) for public sector HE in 1984-5 aimed to improve efficiency and reduce costs (Pratt and Silverman 1988), the effect of which was to lead to massive increases in student numbers from 1979 with reduced levels of resourcing.

The Education Reform Act of 1988 changed HE funding arrangements giving corporate status and responsibility for their finances to Polytechnics. "Higher Education: a new framework" in 1991 (DES) created the means whereby Polytechnics could become Universities. Funding Councils were set up for England, Scotland and Wales and a central quality audit unit was established (Higher Education Quality Council - HEQC). CNAA was to be wound up and institutions would award their own degrees. The paper saw participation rates as likely to continue to increase and that it was in the best interests of all involved to look for increased funding from private sources.

The Polytechnics and Colleges Funding Council (PCFC) paper "Funding Choices" (1989) stated that three factors should influence the allocation of funds to HE: student demand; quality; price. It talked of consumers of HE, such as employers, research councils and the nation, and their capacity to influence HE through the job market, direct talks with the institutions and by persuading the Government. Clearly influenced by "Competence and Competition"(MSC/NEDO, 1984) and the practices of West Germany, Japan and the USA, the Conservative Governments wished to encourage HE to generate income through involvement with employers. The Enterprise in Higher Education Initiative (Training Agency 1990) was very explicit about encouraging employers to contribute to HE. Employers, via the Council for Industry and HE, seemed less enthusiastic about shifting the costs of education onto themselves:

> "A partnership strategy must see industry primarily as a customer rather than a supplier or financier to HE, which must remain a public responsibility to which companies contribute willingly through taxes" (Council for Industry and Higher Education 1987)

In the 1990s there has been an increasing concern with accountability. HEQC in 1995 launched a graduate Standards Programme in response to a request by the Committee of Vice Chancellors and Principals (CVCP) to try to identify standards for undergraduate degrees (HEQC, 1995). This interest in identifying standards has partly resulted from a vast increase in size in HE. The mechanisms which were appropriate for establishing standards when HE was small scale were no longer so. New subjects, methods of delivery and organisation of the curriculum (eg modulerisation) had caused assumptions to be revised, as had the increase in student numbers with reduced resources. Increased collaboration in the UK and internationally between institutions meant a need for greater explicitness (HEQC 1996).

1.4 The context, in summary

A number of assumptions can be discerned in the above accounts. There is the view that the world and its economy is changing rapidly, and that a nation's success is dependent on individuals who are flexible, able to continue to learn and have skills which are transferable between situations. HE is costly and must be justified in terms of its contribution to the economy by developing individuals who can cope successfully with employment. HE must be accountable and justify its value to the country, and part of this must relate to its ability to prove that it is indeed developing the individual "transferable skills" needed to underpin the economy. There are educational justifications for skills approaches, but this paper has focused particulary on the political and economic justifications.

This paper will review terms such as core, key, transferable, or personal skills, will critically review the assumptions identified above, and will then describe relevant educational initiatives.

2 A Critical Review

2.1 What do the terms mean?

A main educational purpose is seen to be to develop in students the capacity to cope successfully, for the benefit of the economy, the nation, and themselves. Education will develop "capability", "competence", "transferable skills", core or key skills. What do these terms mean? They will be explained more fully in the section on national initiatives, but the following brief descriptions and definitions may prove helpful here.

Some examples of definitions and descriptions

Term/topic	Definition/Description	Source
Some general statements on skills	education is concerned with the development of habits, memories, ideas, manual and mental skill, intellectual interests, moral ideals, and in awareness of methods as well as facts.	Spens 1938
	"basic literacy, basic numeracy, the understanding of how to live and work together, respect for others, respect for the individual ......enquiring minds and an appetite for knowledge that will last a lifetime."	Callaghan 1977
	"awareness of the requirements of working life, including particularly how to find and retain suitable employment, and to improve his (sic) social skills, including his (sic) ability to communicate with others orally and to present himself (sic) confidently in interview and group discussions."	Young People at Work MSC 1977
	Self reliance skills. Career management and effective learning skills. Self awareness. Self promotion. Exploring and creating opportunities. Action planning. Networking. Matching and decision making. Negotiation. Policial awareness. Coping with uncertainty. Development focus. Transfer skills. Self-confidence.	Skills for Graduates in the 21st Century. AGR 1995
Capability	emphasises the competence of learners, their capacity to cope, their creative abilities, their ability to cooperate and get on with others.	Education for Capability RSA 1980 NCVQ 1988
Competence	NCVQ has developed the concept of 'competence' - *"something which a person in a given occupational area should be able to do"*	(Training Agency, Guidance Note 2, 1988)

Core/Key Skills	*"communication, problem solving, personal skills, numeracy, information technology and modern language competence"*	National Curriculum Council 1990
	".. values and integrity; effective communication; application of numeracy; application of technology; understanding of work and the world; personal and interpersonal skills; problem solving; positive attitudes to change." (p13)	The Confederation of British Industry (1990)
	Core Skills: Communication Application of number Information technology Personal Skills - Working with others Personal Skills - Improving own learning and performance (Renamed Key Skills in 1996)	National Council for Vocational Qualifications (1996)
	Key skills: Communication Numeracy Information Technology Learning to learn	National Committee of Inquiry into HE (1997)

2.2 Contradictions and dissent

In considering the assumptions underlying the 'Great Debate' it seems useful to consider how far the economy really is dependent upon the skills of individuals, where this focus on the individual comes from, whether or not skills are transferable, and what employers actually want in their graduate recruits.

The economy and people's skills

A 1980 report claimed

> *"It is difficult if not impossible to prove that particular features of a country's education and training system are associated with high or low levels of productivity" (Central Policies Review staff 1980 p3)*

Are those in education and the individuals they teach really responsible for economic performance? In "The Audit of War" Corelli Barnett reviews the reality of Britain as a Great Nation from the time of the industrial revolution, tracing the demise of some of our major industries. He identifies as a major problem our valuing of the "practical man" (sic) to the detriment of scientific and technical expertise.

> *"Coal provides a classic case-study of the survival in Britain of the 'practical man' whose horizon was bounded by the short-term gain; who learned on the job, whether in the boardroom or the manager's office, on the shopfloor or down the mine, by picking up things for himself or acquiring rules-of thumb from his elders; worse perhaps, who learned from his elders traditional attitudes about how to deal with 'the men' or how to fight 'the boss' (Barnett 1986 p68)*

The practical approaches which had been sufficient in the early years of the industrial revolution, when our natural resources gave us a head start on other countries, subsequently proved inadequate but continued to be valued. By the time we realised the importance of scientific and technical education others had passed us by.

> *"Suddenly (1867) the 'practical man' was perceived by enlightened British observers to be no longer adequate ..... there ensued some seventy years of quarter-hearted, piecemeal and always belated improvements in research and education". (Barnett 1986 p98-100)*

Barnett's views on the practical man are echoed elsewhere.

> *"Management in Britain has traditionally been more to do with pragmatism than professionalism. Common sense, character and background have been thought more important than education, with experience the only worthwhile school". (Handy et al 1987 p10)*

Barnett does not identify the inadequacies of individual managers and workers as the sole cause of our economic ills. He talks of the decline in world demand for our traditional products, and the removal of the important protective economic "buffers" of the Empire, then the Commonwealth, and during the second world war, of the USA, whose supplies of steel made our industrial performance look much better than it really was. Industrial organisation was also a major contributing factor.

> *"The main reason for low average British productivity and concomitant high average costs .... over half the total production came out of small and obsolete plants". (Barnett 1986 p88)*

Such is the description of our steel industry before the second world war, whereas in Germany large conglomerates were installing new plant. During the war we were building ships as one-offs while Germany was prefabricating sections for assembly at the shipyards on a production-line basis. British employers tended not to plan ahead, or to innovate whilst their orderbooks were full. After the war nationalisation brought a different set of problems, and Barnett claims that policy making based on strict ideologies (of various political persuasions) also led to our economic malaise.

Our entrenched class system has not helped our economic performance, with historical antagonism between management and workers. Barnett's review of the coal industry is full of allusions to this issue, and in the shipbuilding industry he identifies 'restrictive' practices built up to protect the various crafts from management 'threats' as a major cause for the decline of that industry. Economic performance seems to result from a number of complex factors.

The focus on the individual

An RSA occasional paper suggests that the logical extension of the thinking behind skills approaches in schools was that these schools are responsible for Britain's economic regeneration (Chambers 1986). Gleeson claims that:

> *"By making workers more responsible for their own destinies (epitomised in the term 'on your bike' - Tebbitt 1983; 'taking your skills with you' Hays 1983) ... no recrimination can be made against employers or the state". (Dale ed.1985 p66)*

Finn, another contributor to the same book, adds that

> *"The MSC helped to evolve the mythology that youth unemployment was caused by a mismatch between young workers capacities and the characteristics required by employers". Dale ed. 1985 p118)*

Foucault (1977) provided an interesting perspective on the focus on the individual. He considered that history was determined less by the effect of significant individuals or events than by what the predominant "discourse" of the day. Individuals' actions and historical events are of significance only insofar as the discourse makes them so.

Foucault's use of the word 'discourse' is difficult to translate, but it can be seen as the way individuals in a particular group or society speak to each other and the values and assumptions which are inherent in their communications. Discourses change and develop over time. How does a discourse permeate society? Foucault saw power and knowledge as inextricably linked. For example, teachers are both subject to the power of others, teaching that which is required, but also are the means whereby the required knowledge is transmitted to the pupils or students in their 'power'.

Foucault saw modern western society as disciplining its members by the discourse of individualisation. Discipline is created less by the use of force or by economic restraints, as perhaps during the industrial revolution, than by encouraging individuals to adhere to certain norms. Through the discourse of individualisation individuals, rather than society, are responsible for their own success, and by extension for the success of the nation. Individuals are encouraged to adhere to the norms of the discourse of individualisation in various ways, of which one is 'surveillance'. For example, in order to enter University or certain professions individuals must pass examinations which test whether they meet certain norms. Examinees sit in a room under the observation of invigilators, their work is assessed, and the examiners' work is scrutinised by second markers and external examiners - 'surveillance' at each stage.

Many aspects of the educational debate in which the skills movement is set can be related to 'individualisation'. Employment structures focus increasingly on the individual. Collective bargaining is reduced with individuals negotiating their own working contracts. Modularisation is breaking down the barriers of the traditional disciplines and, theoretically, giving individuals more choice. In HE there has been a shift from a focus on the discipline and knowledge and towards individual skills, and the skills referred to are usually not technical or subject related, but tend to be those associated with the person. HE institutions are increasingly accountable for their individual performance and the performance of students and staff, and surveillance mechanisms are on the increase (HEQC, HEFCE, league tables).

The link made between individuals' skills and national economic performance seems firmly set within Foucault's discourse of individualisation. This is not to say that this discourse is not 'real', indeed its very power makes it real, but it is one perception of reality and one not universally shared.

Are these skills transferable?

The view that skills are transferable has a long pedigree. As we have already seen Newman (1853) considered that University education developed a range of intellectual and personal skills which could be used subsequently.

What do we mean by 'transfer'?

"generally stated (transfer) is the phenomenon of learning more easily or more effectively than otherwise in a new situation as a result of learning which has taken place earlier." (Matthews, 1986 p3)

Matthews takes "near" transfer as being able to repeat a procedure in a new situation, for example changing gear in different cars, and "far" transfer as relating to underlying principles, as when faced with a traffic accident requiring rapid responses in an unexpected situation. It is difficult to measure transfer. The above definition suggests that one way of doing so is to identify how long it takes an individual to manage a task in a new situation, but Matthews suggests that there may be other factors to take into account, such as motivation towards the task.

Oates (1992) claims that there is little research evidence that skills are transferable, yet it is widely assumed that they are.

"One reason why the notion of general transfer keeps arising from the grave is that it is such an attractive proposition for psychologists and educationalists alike. It is the one effect that, if discovered and engineered, could liberate students and teachers from the shackles of narrow, disciplinary education. Sustaining these longings is the fact that it is very difficult to prove that something does not exist. There is always another manipulation in the psychologists tool box to try" (Singley and Anderson 1989 p25)

Neath (1997) claims that in the last decade psychological research has moved from what he describes as a crude debate between near and far transfer and now tends to concentrate on something between the two. Most of the transfer research has been on problem solving, and it has recently focused on applying problem solving skills within a particular domain, rather than more generally. Research on problem solving has tended to be experimental, with a group trained to solve a problem and an untrained control group both given a problem to solve. Research indicates that there is some evidence for near transfer but not for general or far transfer.

The Author's own gathering of student perceptions of their courses suggests that individuals find it difficult to make connections between very different situations where the same skill is needed. Students tend to be unmotivated and puzzled by skills units or modules which are not firmly set within the subject. They find it difficult to identify how interpersonal or communication skills used for traditional academic tasks such as writing essays or participating in seminars might be applicable to work.

Neath's (1997) research into students' acquisition of group work skills indicates the complexity of the transfer issue. A "skill" such as group work is composed of many elements, including attitudes, motivations, personality factors, habitual behaviour and communication techniques. What exactly transfers? Neath finds that context is very important. Lecturers give students group project work to develop inter-personal skills, but Neath found that what students may learn through such work are strategies for maximising their marks and reducing any damaging influence of others on their marks. These strategies may vary between individuals depending, for example, on their preferred way of relating to others. The strategies might be unnecessary and therefore not transferred to group projects which are assessed differently or not assessed at all.

What do employers really want?

> *".... there is a conflict between the explicit statements made by employers and the implicit signals in the way they select and recruit employees" (Central Policy Review Staff 1980 p4)*

Employers claim to be seeking a range of "transferable skills", but their recruitment practices indicate they are very concerned with status. Harvey et al (1997) found that those recruiting graduates (as opposed to recruiting for a specific job) were more likely to

> *"...narrow down the choice on the basis of spurious criteria such as A level grades, degree classification, or reputation of higher education institution". (Harvey et al 1997 p3)*

Harvey et al point out that such practices are unlikely to target the 'transformative employees' organisations need.

Employers are often quoted as a homogeneous group whilst this is not the case. It is particularly difficult to establish the needs of small and medium sized employers (SMEs). For example Smith, Wolstencroft and Southern (1989) found that different employers used the same terms to describe different attributes, echoed by a later Assocation of Graduate Recruiters (AGR) report.

> *"Employers have vastly differing requirements, despite the similarities in language which exist. For example, 'communication skills' will mean very differing things to a publisher and a local government employee.........(Employers) are also unlikely to take account of the need for skills to know how and when to leave a job, not just to find and keep one." (AGR 1995 p 18)*

The AGR report also stated that asking employers what skills they need in graduates is unproductive, as their views are most likely to be based on past requirements rather then a strategic assessment of future needs.

A report by McGeevor and Brennan (1990) claimed that focusing on personal and social attributes may perpetuate social hierarchies and militate against equal opportunities, since socially dominant groups such as employers may emphasise those qualities most valued by themselves rather than those needed at work. Focusing on technical as opposed to personal skills, which are more likely to be influenced by background, is likely to lead to less discrimination against groups such as black students (or presumably women or any disadvantaged group). The 1995 AGR report suggests that as graduate employment with SMEs increases so may the possiblity of discrimination, since recruitment is more unlikely to be carried out by non specialists.

Contradictions and dissent, in summary

There are alternative perceptions of the main assumptions underlying the skills movement. The factors determining economic success are complex and relate to social structures, infrastructures, and ideological policy decisions, as well as to education, training, and individual abilities. The focus on "transferable skills" can be seen as part of the particular discourse of individualisation. Research evidence has not yet made out an effective case for the transferability of broad skills. Employers recruitment practices do not confirm their professed interest in graduates' skills, and a focus on individuals' personal skills may lead to discrimination or to the under-use of those with technical skills and knowledge who perhaps do not conform to the personal norms required.

Skills approaches are, however, becoming embedded within education. They are attractive to educators who may be less immediately motivated by a concern to support the national economy than by a concern to support the development of the whole person, which skills approaches imply.

3 Skills Initiatives

In the 1970s, 80s and 90s a variety of national initiatives aimed to develop skills in individuals and to encourage appropriate teaching and learning strategies. These strategies typically have the following aims:

- to give more responsibility to learners
- to meet the learner's rather than the teacher's needs
- to require active participation by the learner
- to provide links with the 'real world'.

These aims reflect many aspects of the educational literature mentioned in the above section 'The Debate'. For example: Spens (1938) advocated learning through activity and experience and the giving of greater responsibility to pupils; Robbins (1963) was critical of the lecture as the standard means of HE instruction; Faure (1972) described the teacher's role as changing from the authoritative delivery of knowledge to the diagnosis of learners' needs, motivating learners and monitoring progress, and emphasised the value of self-learning and adapting teaching to the learner's needs.

3.1 An introduction to some of the main agencies

Some of the national initiatives were inter-connected, others arose independently. They were often based on innovations in teaching and learning which had arisen for pedagogic reasons, often from ideological standpoints quite different from those of the 'Establishment' which took them over. During the 1980s the Training Agency, part of the Department of Employment (DoE), assumed an increasingly central role. Most Department of Education and Science (DES) funding went directly to Local Education Authorities (LEAs), it retaining only a small amount of development money, whereas the Training Agency had large funds which it could deploy rapidly. The Conservative Administrations tended to promote vocational policies through the latter.

A White Paper "Employment for the 1990s (DoE 1988) initiated the establishment of 80-100 Training and Enterprise Councils (TECs), shifting responsibility for training to local communities and away from the Training Agency, which became a policy making body. TECs are related to a particular location, employer-led, concerned with business growth, focus on performance and enterprise and have targetted approaches. The Sheffield TEC's mission statement, for example, is:

> *"To improve the economic prosperity and quality of life in Sheffield through a training and enterprise partnership and investment in people" (Sheffield TEC 1997)*

Sheffield TEC's annual report (1997) refers to its support for a range of training initiatives: employers meeting certain criteria are acknowledged as 'Investors in People'; Modern Apprenticeships and National Vocational Qualifications (NVQs); schemes linking employment and education, such as the Teacher Placement Service (10% of teachers in the city were placed with local businesses in 1995/6) and Work Experience for pre 16 year olds.

In September 1996 the Department for Education and Employment was created, merging the old DoE and DES, and this symbolises the connection increasingly being made between education and employment.

3.2 Some developments in schools

Educational developments in schools in recent years have been characterised by:

- new forms of assessment (continuous assessment, criterion referencing, profiling, Records of Achievement)
- active learning
- changes in the teaching role and shifts of responsibility from teacher to pupil
- a curriculum more relevant to "real life"
- greater contact whilst at school with "real life situations".

As early as the 1960s Nuffield Science was using active learning strategies. Several innovations during the early 1970s became major elements of national schemes by the 1980s, for example profiling and a scheme where pupils made and recorded statements about their work.

The Waddell report (1978) advocated replacing the GCE and CSE by one examination where the curriculum defined the examination and not vice versa and where continuous assessment by teachers, which Waddell thought most effective in acknowledging skills and learning, would predominate over externally assessed written examinations. The GCSE was announced by the Government in June 1984, introduced in 1986 and the first pupils were assessed in 1988. GCSE aims to cater for the majority of pupils, and its predominant modes of assessment are criterion referenced, continuous and allow for the testing of skills.

"Better Schools" (DES 1985) initiated the national curriculum, claiming that schools should motivate pupils towards active rather than passive learning and listing curricular objectives which included skill development for a rapidly changing world. The curriculum should be broad, balanced, relevant and matched to student's abilities and attitudes, and the teaching role should be one of organising and creating situations where pupils can learn. Teaching methods should enable the development and demonstration of qualities such as working co-operatively, perseverance, the acceptance of responsibility and an enterprising attitude.

The Education Reform Act of 1988 established the framework for the national curriculum (NC). The paper Choice and Diversity (DfE and Welsh Office, 1992) claimed that the debate had moved on from whether there should be a NC to what should be in it. The NC sets national targets for 5 -16 year olds in key subjects, with tests at 7, 11, 14 and 16 which are criterion referenced and, it is claimed, therefore comparable across the country.

The National Record of Achievement (NRA) was launched in 1991. It includes both formative and summative elements, involves self assessment, and aims to provide pupils with a record of personal achievements, skills and qualities, and academic attainments. The National Council for Vocational Qualifications (NCVQ) and Scotvec are responsible for developing and marketing the NRA. Dearing (1996) in his review of qualifications for 16-19 year olds, claims its greatest success has been in schools, where over 80% of pupils at year 11 use it. Dearing recommended a relaunch of the scheme to address certain problems: it should be introduced earlier when pupils select their final 2 compulsory years of education; it should have a greater role in personal development; there should be training for pupils in using it with employers; it should have a major role in developing skills and be linked to the 'Improving Own Learning and Performance' NCVQ Core Skill (see later section on Core/Key Skills).

The Higginson Report of 1988 recommended a reform of A levels to bring them more into line with GCSE:

- a broader range of subjects
- assessment to provide feedback into teaching and learning rather than purely an end exam
- active learning
- more relevance
- the use of non-textbook information.

This Report was rejected by the Government, but the CBI's "Towards a Skills Revolution" (1989) supported its recommendations. Dearing (1996) thought A levels were generally respected and fulfilled an important role in developing information and critical evaluation skills, and did not recommend major changes. However he recommended that A level syllabuses be reviewed to see where Key Skills (see later section) could be built in and also the introduction of an A/S level in Key Skills, which universities should support by taking account of it in selecting students.

Another major development is in the increase in contacts between schools and employers and the community, through work and community experience schemes such as Compact, where an employer provides work experience and pupils set themselves individual personal targets (Scottish Office 1991). In the 70s and 80s there was considerable growth in industrial liaison.

"The Schools Industry Liaison Officer (SILO) nearly always an employee of the local education authority, acts as broker, adviser and facilitator .... The rise of the SILO has been dramatic. The first recorded post was in 1966 (Wood 1983); by 1985 three quarters of all LEAs had one". (Dale ed 1985 p34)

Currently Education Business Partnerships promote awareness between schools and employment and Compact schemes are integrated within them. In 1995-6 Sheffield TEC placed 4,900 pupils, for example (Sheffield TEC, 1997).

3.3 Some developments in Further Education

Skills approaches in FE can be traced to the early 1970s when FE colleges in London amalgamated to produce a smaller number of colleges (Waugh 1988). The report leading to this amalgamation considered General Studies work in a way which led to a focus on communication skills. There had been a tradition of student centred work and some London general education teachers had been meeting informally since 1971 to develop workshop approaches and resource-based learning. This was subsequently supported by intensive staff development and several of them became advisory teachers. Waugh claims that one reason behind the 1970s communication skills movement was university-educated general education teachers attempting to secure a better footing in colleges dominated by technical teachers, within the context of merging colleges.

In 1977 the Further Education Curriculum Research and Development Unit (FEU) was established including staff with General Studies backgrounds. The FEU, now named the Further Education Development Agency (FEDA), produces a wide range of documents and organises events about educational issues in FE, pre-dominantly advocating student-centred approaches. Its work, for example, influenced the development of the Certificate of Pre Vocational Education (CPVE) described below.

3.4 The new training initiative (NTI)

The NTI (MSC 1981) was extremely influential. It advocated: training for skills; planned work experience or full-time education for all those under 18; more access for adults to VET; building on existing programmes such as the Youth Opportunities Programme (YOP), Unified Vocational Preparation (UVP) Training for Skills (TSPA) and Training Opportunities (TOPS).

"The new markets and technologies required a more highly skilled better educated and more mobile workforce" (MSC 1981 p.2)
"For too long we have treated training and education as a once for all experience at the start of life" (MSC 1981 p.3)

It is within the NTI that reference begins to be made to the standards of competence which were to become the central focus for the NCVQ. The NTI was clear that a major shake-up of our VET systems was needed and that employers must bear most of the cost of training. Most of the following initiatives can be traced back to the NTI.

3.5 The technical and vocational educational initiative (TVEI)

TVEI was announced by the Government in 1982. A 'vision statement' described its role:

"..to help produce a more highly skilled competent, effective and enterprising workforce for the 1990s. It is a bold long-term strategy, unique amongst nations, for investing in the skill of all our young people 14 - 18 in full-time education and equipping them for the demands of working life in a rapidly changing highly technological society.
It does this by
* *relating what is learnt in schools and colleges to the world of work*
* *improving the skills and qualifications for all; in particular in science, technology, information technology and modern languages*
* *providing young people with direct experience of the world of work through real work experience*
* *enabling young people to be effective, enterprising and capable at work through active and practical learning methods*
* *providing counselling, guidance, individual action plans, records of achievement and opportunities to progress to higher levels of achievement.*
The vision
The long term goal is that all students leaving full-time initial education at whatever age should be equipped with the knowledge, skills and qualities needed in the workplace of tomorrow. Each should have an individual action plan and a record of achievement suitable for use by employers or Further/ Higher Education Institutions. The record of achievement, of simple and standard form, would be compatible with NROVA and record personal qualities as well as qualifications and other relevant information. This record would be built on throughout adult and working life" (Training Agency 1990)

The NROVA is the National Record of Vocational Achievement renamed the National Record of Achievement (NRA)

There were 14 small TVEI pilots in 1982 and from 1984 participating LEAs were given £2 million per project for 5 years by the Manpower Services Commission (renamed the Training Agency, then renamed the Training Education and Enterprise Directorate - TEED, now the Department for Education and Employment).

"It marked the first direct intervention of the MSC (now the Training Agency) in schools provision, and was unusual in that the contract was between MSC and LEAs" (FEU 1989 p1)

LEAs submitted varied proposals, but all were concerned with the development of the curriculum, teaching/ learning strategies and staff development. The extension of TVEI to all schools was announced in 1986 in "Working Together - Education and Training (DoE and DES) and all extensions had to comply with the aims for education outlined in "Better Schools" (DES 1985). Common elements were profiling, certification, negotiation between pupils and teachers, experiential learning, and breaking down traditional divisions between subjects.

When funding ends in 1997 the scheme will have cost £1 billion (Hudson 1996). Although TVEI is no longer an initiative as such, the term is still used. Work experience is a main aspect and it is likely that Government funding for this will continue, although Hudson (1996) indicates that linking work experience into the curriculum has always been problematic.

"It was as though their (politicians and civil servants) reasoning had led them to the conclusion that pupils very experience of work would, by osmosis, achieve its aims of the experience" (Hudson, 1996, p279)

3.6 The certificate of pre-vocational education (CPVE)

CPVE resulted from proposals by the DES that the Business and Technical Education Council (BTEC) and City and Guilds of London Institute (CGLI) develop a new vocational qualification. The new programmes began in 1985. BTEC and CGLI claimed that CPVE would provide programmes:

"relevant to the needs of young people as emerging adults and prospective employees. The curriculum of such courses must include not only the acquisition of knowledge and analytical and creative skills, but also constructive creative activity which involves putting ideas into practice, making, doing and organising." (Joint Board 1984)

It would contain a common core of personal and career development, communication, numeracy, science and technology, skills for learning, decision making and adaptability, practical skills, social skills and creative development. CPVE was intended to provide 16 year olds in FE with a flexible programme including formal qualifications, such as GCSE and to enable students to sample employment. It aimed to aid:

"the transition from school to adulthood,... provide individually relevant educational experience learning and achievement ... to provide young people with ... a qualification which embodies national standards ... to provide opportunities for progression" (Morning 1988 p.9)

Assessment was negotiated by student and tutor, based on profiling using competency statements. By 1988 10% of 16 year olds in full-time education in England and Wales were on CPVE programmes. In the late 1980s CPVE evolved into the CGLI administered Diploma of Vocational Education, itself replaced by GNVQ.

3.7 Youth training (YT)

CPVE and the Youth Training Scheme (YTS) were major influences on FE. Arising out of the NTI, YTS, which began in 1983, was based on a small scheme set up by Yorkshire and Humberside Association of Further and Higher Education called Tradec, itself part of the UVP, a small joint MSC and DES scheme for 16-18 year olds with only 2,500 young participants throughout the country. It was Tradec, which ran from 1976, which provided the design framework for YTS rather than the Youth Opportunities Programme. The latter was devised to deal with a crisis in youth unemployment rather than to provide systematic training. YTS consisted of a mix of training at work and attendance at college and had a strong skills orientation.

The 2 year YTS, launched in 1986, aimed to give each participant an opportunity to obtain a vocational qualification. YTS was one of the influences behind the establishment of NCVQ, since it exposed a serious gap in training provision, with cohorts of YTS trainees joining an employment market with no clear lines of progression. In 1990 the scheme was renamed Youth Training (YT) and became more flexible, guaranteeing places for those aged 16-18 not in full time education or employment. Participants gain a mix of work, with employers funded to offer them places, and training in FE colleges, aiming to reach NVQ 2 (see later section on NCVQ).

Dearing (1996) considered that although the principle of YT is valuable, in practice it is associated with unemployment and some participants are motivated only by receiving benefit. There is a completion rate of 45% and an unemployment rate of 22% six months after completion (Dearing, 1996 p37). Dearing made a number of suggestions, such as renaming the scheme to remove associations with unemployment benefit, including the acquisition of Key Skills as well as NVQs (see later sections), and using the NRA to record employment related evidence such as attendance.

3.8 The core skills project

A major attempt to define more closely what is meant by 'transferable skills' was the MSC (later the Training Agency, later TEED, now DfEE) financed Core Skills Project of 1982-1985. Whilst it focused on the Youth Training scheme (YTS), it aimed to develop a model applicable to all work areas and was concerned with work-based learning, rather than learning through institutionalised courses. It tried to create a common language for skills which could be used and understood by all those involved in Vocational Education and Training (VET), identifying 103 core skills clustered in 14 skill groups, relating to the core areas of number, communication, problem solving and practical.

> *"The core skills are defined as those skills which are common to a wide range of tasks and which are essential for competence in those tasks" (Levy 1987 p.7).*

Level of attainment would depend on the work context, and the project differentiated between those skills which are transferable and those which enable transfer. Any work activity could be analysed in order to identify the core skills used. For example:

> *"Working with people*
> *8.1 Notice when to ask other people in the work-place for assistance (eg noticing when people are too busy to help)*
> *8.2 Ask other people in the work place for assistance*
> *8.3 Notice the need of customers, clients and other people in the workplace eg that people are in difficulty; that customers are waiting for the offer of help or want to be left alone" (Morning 1988 p.9)*

The Project produced a list of 35 key words relating to the core skills groups. For example:

"Core Skills Groups   *Keywords*
1. Operating with numbers   *Count*
                                      Work out
                                      Check and correct
                                      Compare"
                                      (Levy & Matthews 1989 p29)

The Project claimed that the core skills might:

"..be helpful in devising elements of competence and performance criteria, as required for National Vocational Qualifications (NVQ) and other qualifications." (Levy & Matthews 1989 p3).

3.9 The qualifications and curriculum authority (QCA)

The establishment of the National Council for Vocational Qualifications (NCVQ) was announced in the White Paper "Working Together - Education and Training" (DoE and DES 1986) and can be traced back to the 1981 NTI. In October 1997 NCVQ, together with the Schools Curriculum and Assessment Authority (SCAA) became the QCA. NCVQ (now QCA) aimed to rationalise vocational qualifications, create a structure of recognised qualifications understood by everybody and replace the plethora of levels offered by bodies such as RSA, CGLI and BTEC, who would continue to offer qualifications but within the NCVQ framework and accredited by NCVQ. NCVQ also aimed to:

* improve the quality of VET
* aid progression, with access to VET beginning at school
* be responsive to the labour market
* recognise competence and achievement
* give value for money.

By 1991 Industry Lead Bodies were established, each representing a major industry, to define the industry's parameters and agree standards of competence for occupations. NVQs are modular, with employees proving competence at certain levels and accumulating credit, and with credits transferable to other occupations. There were initially 4 levels of NVQ with a fifth professional level introduced early in 1990. NCVQ acknowledged the complexity of defining competence at this fifth level.

"Competence in the pursuit of a senior occupation or profession - as an employee or as a self-employed person - including the ability to apply a significant range of fundamental principles and techniques to diagnosis, planning and problem solving. Extensive knowledge and understanding will be required to underpin competence at this level, together with capability in management and supervision for executive and some professional fields" (NCVQ 1989 p5).

NCVQ attempted to map its levels against academic qualifications, so that level 2 is comparable to GCSE, level 3 to A Level, level 4 to final year degree (but not to graduation) level, and 5 to professional qualifications.

The NCVQ attempted to define competence and standards.

> *"Standards are based on the needs of employment and embody the skills and knowledge, and the level of performance relevant to the work activity." (Guidance Note 1 Training Agency 1988).*

Competence is a

> *"..wide concept which embodies the ability to transfer skills and knowledge to new situations within the occupational area" (Guidance Note 1 Training Agency 1988)*

and

> *"..something which a person in a given occupational area should be able to do ...." (Guidance Note 2),*

An element of competence is

> *"..what can be done; an action behaviour or outcome which a person should be able to demonstrate." (Guidance Note 1 Training Agency 1988)*

Competence consists of 4 components -
> *"task skills*
> *task management skills*
> *contingency management skills (for when things go wrong)*
> *job/role environment skills (such as working relationships)". (Guidance Note 2 Training Agency 1988)*

Elements of competence are arrived at by "functional analysis" i.e.

> *"..describe the key purpose of the occupational area - ask what needs to happen for this to be achieved - repeat the process until the functions being identified are a unit level - repeat the process for each unit until the functions are at unit level ". (Guidance Note 2 Training Agency 1988)*

NCVQ claimed that assessing an individual's competence by collecting evidence about performance and judging it against standards was a radical departure from traditional practice. Vocational qualifications are no longer awarded on the basis of time served or examined knowledge but on on-the-job performance.

In addition to NVQs, NCVQ developed the General National Vocational Qualification (GNVQ), which aims to provide a *"valuable alternative"* (NCVQ 1995) to GCE A level.

> *"GNVQs provide a broad based vocational education which continues many aspects of general education. As well as acquiring the basic skills and broad knowledge which underpin a vocational area, all students have to achieve core skills. The attainment of both vocational and core skills provides a foundation from which students can progress either to further and higher education or into employment and further training" (NCVQ 1995)*

GNVQs became available in 1993 and by 1994 164,000 students were registered. There are 3 levels, Foundation, Intermediate and Advanced, which equate with NVQ levels 1-3 and where the Advanced level is equivalent in standard to GCE A level. The core skills (see later section) of Communication, Application of Number and IT are mandatory to GNVQ, and Personal Skills are promoted in additional units. GNVQs are unit based, allow for credit accumulation, and are composed of core skill and vocational units. Students provide evidence of their attainment of specified learning outcomes, evidence coming from projects, assignments and other course activities.

3.10 The business and technical education council (BTEC)

BTEC was formed in 1983 when the Business Education Council and the Technician Education Council merged. In September 1996 it became part of Edexcel along with London Examinations. BTEC aims to improve the quality of work-related education and to improve students' competence in their careers for the good of themselves, their employers and the nation. Its "Policies and Priorities into the 1990s" (1984) was produced against the background of the NTI and resulted from a high level "think-tank" of industrialists, educators and professionals, with the need for flexible workforce as its major impetus.

In 1986, BTEC began to require all courses to grade "common skills": self development skills; communicating and working with others; problem tackling; decision making and investigating; information, quantitative and numerical skills; practical skills. BTEC produced specific guidelines for course teams and would only approve courses which complied with them. Although staff and students often found the requirements onerous, BTEC's skills approach has had a considerable influence on teaching and learning strategies in BTEC courses which have often spilled over onto degree programmes in the same departments.

During 1990 BTEC developed a competence based framework for common skills to fit with the NCVQ approach and the 16-19 core skills proposed by the National Curriculum Council in March 1990. BTEC was also influenced by the CBI report "Towards a Skills Revolution" (1990) which was concerned with *"action for bridging the skills gap"* (CBI 1990 p9), specifically for 14 - 18 year olds. From September 1991 the following 'transferable skills' had to be assessed in all its qualifications, regardless of vocational area:

- managing and developing self
- communicating
- working with and relating to others
- managing tasks and solving problems
- applying technology.

Some BTEC national certificates and diplomas have been replaced by GNVQs, and here core/key skills are assessed (see later section) rather than common skills.

3.11 Education for capability

The Education for Capability manifesto, published in 1978 by the Royal Society for the Encouragement of Arts, Manufacture and Commerce (RSA) claimed that there is an imbalance in education and training. Whilst the majority of learners will engage in practical lives the ideal of the scholarly person is of an individual who thinks rather than acts. In an RSA occasional paper Charles Handy advocates an education system which is more like a marathon than a horse race.

"In a mass marathon everyone who completes the course wins, although some run faster than others". (Handy 1984 p3)

A programme which 'educates for capability' should lead through active learning to increased competence and capacity to cope. Whereas NVQs identify discrete elements of competence combining to form a competent individual, 'capability' is a more holistic concept referring to the capacities of a person in total, interests, skills and experience all being of significance. The criteria underpinning any Education for Capability programme, include:

- active learning
- reference to problems relevant to people's lives
- accessibility for a wide range of learners
- negotiating between teachers and learners. (RSA 1980)

The movement developed a recognition scheme for programmes meeting its criteria, organised conferences and seminars and produced newsletters. In 1988, it launched Higher Education for Capability (HEC).

> *"Higher Education for Capability is looking for much broader concepts of 'relevance' than is implied by 'entrepreneurialism'". (Stephenson 1988 p3)*

HEC organises national and regional events each with a focus on a particular aspect of capability (eg assessment for capability), produces a journal and supports a network of university staff.

3.12 Enterprise in Higher Education (EHE)

EHE was launched in December 1987 and ran until December 1996. HE Institutions bid for up to £1 million each for a 5 year period in which to bring about change leading to the development of more enterprising qualities in students.

> *"..the enterprising person is resourceful, adaptable, creative, innovative and dynamic. He or she may also be entrepreneurial. However the qualities of enterprise are as useful in the employee as in the employer, and equally important in the public, private and voluntary sectors". (Training agency 1990 p3)*

The funding was pump priming, with the intention that each institution's programme would be self-financing by the end of 5 years. A key feature was that students engage in real life situations, with employers contributing either in kind or financially and participating in assessment. As a result of the programme students should

> *"..be more enterprising, have developed transferable skills, be more realistically informed about employment opportunities, aims and challenges and make better career choices, be better prepared to take responsibility in their professional and working lives." (Training Agency 1990 p4)*

EHE was intended not as an add-on but as an influence on the whole curriculum throughout the institution. It claimed as its influences TVEI, CPVE, Mini Enterprise Projects, Education for Capability and YTS. Projects varied since:

> *"Institutions tended to define enterprise in ways that reflect their values and traditions". (TA 1990 p5)*

However, an Employment Department report stated that

"there has been a convergence around the transferable skills definition of enterprise". (Employment Department 1991)

and Binks (1996) claims that skills development was a central feature of EHE programmes. Significant other common features have included:

- the appointment of individuals with responsibility for coordinating the programme
- work placements or shadowing
- project work
- involvement with students unions
- partnership with companies
- active learning
- accreditation and assessment
- learning contracts
- a significant focus on staff development.

3.13 UDACE project on learning outcomes

In the spring of 1990 a two year Training Agency funded project led by the Unit for the Development of Adult and Continuing Education (UDACE), since merged with FEDA, attempted to define learning outcomes and pilot their assessment for five disciplines in HE (English; Social Science; Engineering; Environmental Studies; Design), involving three HE institutions for each discipline (Otter 1992). The Project gathered information in an attempt to fill each of the following boxes.

	Expected Learning Outcomes	**Actual Learning Outcomes**
Students		
Academic Staff		
Employers		

The project reflected growing Training Agency interest in clarifying outcomes rather than prescribing the content of education and training or the processes by which it takes place. The project was extremely influential and there is now a widespread use in universities of learning outcomes.

3.14 Credit accumulation and transfer schemes (CATS) and the accreditation of prior experiential learning (APEL)

Since 1986 HE institutions have adopted CATS, whereby students build credit for completing parts of courses to add up to a complete qualification. The scheme fits in with the themes of transfer and accumulating credit notable in the work of NCVQ, and it may also contain the option of claiming credit for prior experiential learning, for example through work, in which not only knowledge but the demonstration of ability and skills may count. It is a mechanism for extending access and facilitating the lifelong learning advocated by Faure and others.

3.15 QCA key skills

The term "key skills" has been used since Dearing's 1996 report, before which they were referred to as "core skills".

> *"They are the skills which are common and applicable to a wide range of contexts and are an important part of effective performance in those contexts. Core Skills offer the potential for enhancing transfer of learning to new contexts, not least by making people more aware of the skills that they possess and of the skills which are required in different contexts". (Oates 1992 p11)*

In February 1989 the Secretary of State for Education outlined the merits of incorporating Core Skills in all post 16 education and training, including A/AS levels and NVQs. This was endorsed by the CBI (1989), which offered a tentative list of such skills, and also by the TUC (1989). The National Curriculum Council (NCC) was asked by the Secretary of State to consult with the Schools Assessment and Examination Council (SEAC), the Council for National Academic Awards (CNAA) and the Further Education Unit (FEU) and to report on Core Skills for A/AS levels.

The NCC in "Core Skills 16 - 19" (1990) proposed that specifications be drawn up for communication, problem solving, personal skills, numeracy, information technology, and competence in a foreign language. Of these, communication, problem solving and personal skills should be present in all Post 16 programmes, numeracy and IT should be present where appropriate, and competence in a modern foreign language should be an entitlement but not a necessity.

SEAC was then asked to report on Core Skills in A/AS levels and NCVQ (now Qualifications and Curriculum Authority - QCA, formed in October 1997 from NCVQ and SCAA) on Core Skills in NVQs, both bodies reporting in 1990. SEAC felt that it might be possible to integrate communication, problem solving and personal skills in A/As levels, but that personal skills might be difficult to assess. NCVQ felt that units could be developed at progressive levels for all Core Skills and that whilst communication, problem solving and personal skills would be relevant to all NVQs, numeracy and IT would be relevant to particular ones. Both bodies stressed that Core Skills must be relevant to and not detract from the qualifications they were to be part of.

A task group, including SEAC and NCVQ, was established to develop Core Skill specifications. In 1991 they produced draft definitions, omitting reference to a foreign language until the publication of the NCC's work on languages. Later in 1991 NCVQ involved CGLI, BTEC, RSA, and SCOTVEC in developing the Core Skills framework and suggested dropping the foreign language because of the danger of overlap with the work of the Languages Lead Body. NCVQ tested their draft specifications on FE colleges, 6th form centres, schools and city technical colleges.

The task group felt that Core Skills should be applicable to all academic and vocational settings and there should be a relationship between the levels and the NCC Attainment Targets. The DES and TEED instructed NCVQ to synchronise Core Skill levels with GNVQ levels, so that Core Skills at level 3 would appear in GNVQ at level 3, and to pursue personal skills and problem solving but not to include them in GNVQ, because of difficulties in assessment.

There was developed, therefore, a 5 level Core Skill framework. NCVQ formally approved the specifications for Communication, Application of Number, and IT in 1992. Core Skills are relevant to all post 16 education and training, but they have been most specifically developed by NCVQ and have initially been incorporated into GNVQ. NCVQ considered that *"there will be a natural evolution of the incorporation of the Core Skills Units into NVQs"* (Oates 1992) and by 1996 some NVQs were incorporating core skills units. In 1995 the specifications for Communication Application of Number and IT were revised, and Personal Skills were revised in 1996. Whilst NCVQ produced specifications in 1992 for Problem Solving, it has not been formally adopted as a Core Skill. For GNVQ the three mandatory Core Skills (now named Key Skills) are assessed as an integral part of the qualification rather than as separate units, but Personal Skills can be included in a GNVQ as an optional element. BTEC, CGLI, and RSA also accredit Key Skills as independent units. Of these RSA has included Problem Solving as a unit (RSA 1997). The list of Key skills is therefore:

- Communication
- Application of number
- Information Technology
- Personal skills - Working with Others
- Personal skills - Improving own Learning and Performance

The design of the key skill units

In developing the specifications NCVQ (now QCA) looked at 24 skills frameworks, the analysis of which led them to conclude that they needed: a robust model with *"secure definitions"* of the skills (Oates 1992 p24); elements amenable to criterion referenced/ outcomes based assessment; a coherent model of skill transfer; specifications at progressive levels; a minimum of overlap between the skills. Of these requirements the one which has been least addressed seems to be the transfer of skills, referred to mainly in terms of making skills explicit and practising them in various contexts.

In particular the developers based their work on the BTEC Common Skills, the CPVE core, the MSC work based learning skills (Tim Oates, head of the development team, worked on the 1982 - 5 Core Skills Project) and innovations in GCSE and A levels. The units build on NVQ work by including elements, performance criteria, range statements and evidence requirements. The Core Skills were designed to be capable of integration into NVQ and GNVQ, to match the specifications explored for A/AS levels and to be appropriate for credit accumulation. They would cover aspects which are common and equally applicable to different occupations and which would complement vocationally specific elements, rather than displace them. Oates claims that they

"are essential to and are embedded within effective performance by an individual". *(1992 p34)*

but that it is still important to highlight them, to ensure they are acquired, to make them explicit and to encourage transfer.

The Core Skills partly overlap with the National Curriculum and are broadly correlated in level, for example Communication overlaps with the subject of English but is not identical to it. The 'broad equivalence' is as follows:

Core (now Key) Skill	National Curriculum
level 1	level 4 and below
level 2	level 5 and 6
level 3	level 7
level 4	level 8 and 9
level 5	level 10 and above

Similarly Key Skills levels are 'broadly equivalent' to NVQ, although the latter are more vocationally specific, so that the IT Core Skill level 3 would be less occupationally specific than an NVQ in the same subject area at level 3.

Each Key Skill is based on a different model, and on differing ways of looking at progression through the 5 levels, but the developers did consider progression generally in the following terms:

- an increase in the number of elements
- a change in the nature of the elements
- a change in the range (ie the contexts in which they are used)
- a change in the performance criteria
- a change in evidence requirements.

Communication was seen as having two main elements: interpreting language; using language to present ideas and information. The developers adopted the notion of "language codes" which are shared by individuals, for example in the same occupational area, and which may need to be altered for different audiences. They also used the notion of "transaction". Does the recipient of a communication understand by it what was intended and does the communicator realise how it has been interpreted? Progression would be indicated by *"the increasing sophistication of performance required by more complex communicative activities" (Oates 1992 p20)*. They considered the following dimensions:

- the nature of the communication
- the structure of the communication
- the nature of the audience
- the need for evaluation.

Although not yet approved, Problem Solving has been specified as a Core/Key Skill. The specification focuses on the extent to which a problem is open or closed, so that at the lower levels problem solving is prescribed (important for safety procedures) and at the higher levels it is open and less structured. The developers considered whether: the problem is defined or needs clarification; the approach is provided or to be selected; the criteria for judging solutions are selected for or by the individual. The dimensions considered were:

- the need for the individual to investigate the problem
- the characteristics of the problem
- choices over which approach to use
- the evaluation of solutions.

Personal Skills were seen as difficult to assess because they overlap with the other Key skills and because values and attitudes are explicitly involved. The important aspects to consider would be promoting diversity, modes of learning, action planning and increasing autonomy. The developers focused on two themes to avoid the danger of overlap. These are given below, together with their dimensions.

Working with Others:

- the need by individuals to negotiate responsibilities in working with others
- the need for individuals to determine working arrangements
- the extent to which feedback is provided on own or other performance
- the need to set goals.

Improving Own Learning and Performance:

* proposing targets for improved learning and performance
* the use of different types of learning activity
* selecting learning strategies
* seeking out feedback and support.

The developers of Application of Number found helpful the concepts of "mathematising", expressing problems in terms of numbers, and "demathematising", taking numerical results and translating them into practical solutions. They attempted to link their work to the National Curriculum Attainment Targets. Progression would be identified by increasing complexity of mathematical operations and by how much guidance is needed. The dimensions considered were:

* gathering and processing data
* representing and tackling problems
* interpreting and presenting data.

Information Technology was seen as quite different from the other areas, a tool performing practical tasks which changes as technology changes. Progression would be identified though increasing breadth in using IT and increasing complexity in the operations performed. The dimensions considered were:

* the complexity of operations to input data
* the complexity of operations to edit/organise data
* presenting information
* evaluating the suitability of IT tools.

The Dearing reports and core/key skills

In his Review of Qualifications for 16-19 year olds (1996) Dearing refers to Communication, Application of Number and IT as "key skills", although his term is now used to refer to all the QCA core skills (RSA 1997). He also sees the ability to *'manage one's learning'* as crucial

> *"In a society which needs increasingly to be committed to life-long learning that last is a key to the rest"*
> *(Dearing 1996 p46)*

Dearing's consultations for the report found that the most frequently expressed concerns were to improve Communication and Application of Number, with few concerns about IT, which schools had successfully integrated into the curriculum. Dearing acknowledges a long history of complaints about numeracy and literacy (quoting reports from 1876, 1925, 1961, 1975). There should be an emphasis on key skills pre 16, but the 16-19 age group must be able to practice and update their skills and learn to use them in context. Dearing quotes a 1995 FE Funding Council report which found cause for concern in the majority of colleges inspected over the development and assessment of the key skills, for example skills required in HE courses, such as note taking and essay writing were not addressed in GNVQ.

Dearing's recommendations included:

* all schools should offer IT qualifications to pupils
* A levels should be reviewed to see how key skills could be built in

- there should be a separate non-mandatory A/S in key skills
- QCA should consider common standards for key skills at A/S level and Advanced GNVQ
- QCA should develop tests for key skills
- there should be discussions with Lead Bodies to see if key skills should be incorporated into NVQs (they are already part of Modern Apprenticeships)
- commitment to key skills should be a priority (for example all young people on publicly funded programmes should develop key skills).

Dearing treats the other core skills separately, but he recommends that all learners should have an opportunity to develop them and they should be incorporated into the NRA.

In his report on Higher Education (NCIHE 1997) Dearing widens the list of key skills from those indicated in his report on 16-19 education (communication, numeracy and IT), to include "learning how to learn". He sees much evidence of support for the development of these skills through HE.

"We see these as necessary outcomes of all higher education programmes" (NCIHE 1997 paragraph 38)

Dearing's recommendations include that:

- programme specifications have intended outcomes in terms of knowledge, key skills, cognitive and subject specific skills.
- there be a focus at institutional level on the development and use of IT, the report considering that the UK already has a good IT infrastructure (eg by the year 2005/06 all students to be required to have access to their own portable computer, all staff to be trained in the use of IT etc)
- admissions procedures should value good levels of competence in communication, numeracy and IT
- students should have a "Progress File" which would enable them to monitor, build and reflect on their personal development
- HEQC should develop with institutions standards for HE qualifications (presumably including key skill standards)
- postgraduate training should be reviewed to include the development of professional skills such as communication, self management and planning.

3.16 Skills approaches in HE

Skills development has always been a feature of HE courses. Newman (1853), for example, thought university developed intellectual, personal, social and moral attributes in students. However skills development has often not been explicit or acknowledged, although this varied between subjects. The Author's own English degree course in the 1960s made no explicit reference to skills, whilst friends on language or science courses undertook activities which were more obviously skills related. HE lecturers often claim that they have always developed skills in students, but their students may not have been aware of this. The Author's experience, as an HE careers adviser, of students who were unable to identify the employable skills acquired on their courses led her to initiate, with a colleague, the Personal Skills and Qualities (PSQ) Project in her own institution in 1987.

Skills became more explicitly part of HE discourses in the mid to late 1980s. In 1987 two separate institution-wide initiatives began in the city of Sheffield which, to the Author's knowledge, were the first in the country, the Personal Skills Unit at the University of Sheffield (ref) and the PSQ Project at Sheffield City Polytechnic (now Sheffield Hallam University). Both, using differing methods, encouraged their institutions to integrate skills approaches within the curriculum. Shortly after these initiatives began came Enterprise in Higher Education, also in 1987. As we have seen this initiative, affecting 60 institutions, had as its major focus the development of 'transferable skills'.

In 1997 the Learning and Teaching Institute of Sheffield Hallam University conducted a survey of HE institutions asking about their practices in skills approaches (research by Phil Bannister, unpublished). One of the questions was whether there was a framework or listing of skills used on an institution-wide basis. Of 32 returned questionnaires, 5 of which were from 'old' or 'established' universities, 17 replied that their institution did not use a skills framework, 12 had their own institutional skills framework, 2 used either the SEEC skills framework or a modification of it and 1 used a modification of the QCA key skills framework. The SEEC framework was developed by the South East England Consortium and includes the skill areas of psychomotor, self appraisal/reflection, planning and management of learning, problem solving, communication and persuasion, and interactive and group skills (Thames Valley University May 1997).

This survey does suggest a commitment to skills development in many institutions, although most respondents were from 'new' universities. There seems to be a preference for 'home grown' definitions and descriptions of skills. At Sheffield Hallam University the QCA skills framework is widely used but not formally adopted by the institution, following an attempt to gain Academic Board approval for this in 1995. Concerns voiced within Sheffield Hallam may account for so many institutions having their own framework, such as the concern that the QCA skills do not address cognitive skills (see the earlier reference to the work of Harvey et al who found that cognitive skills such as criticism and synthesis are important in 'transformative employees'). Cognitive skills are actually contained within the QCA specifications, for example they include evaluation, but not as separate items. There is also a reluctance to repeat the BTEC experience, which was seen as prescriptive and time consuming.

Examples of models used within institutions are:

De Montfort (Walker 1995)

Managing tasks and solving problems	*1 focusing on achieving key objectives*
	2 using analytical and conceptual thinking
	3 gathering information to assist problem solving
	4 making decisions
Working with others	*5 using logical and rational arguments to persuade others*
	6 understanding and building/reflecting on how others perceive him/her
	7 identifying the needs of others and building positive relationships
Communication	*8 oral communication*
	9 written communication
Self awareness	*10 taking responsibility for own learning and development*
	11 dealing with pressure and emotions
	12 showing sense of purpose

Oxford Brookes (Jenkins 1997)

1 *Self management. This refers to a student's general ability to manage her own learning environment.*
2 *Learning skills. This refers to a student's general ability to learn effectively and be aware of her own learning abilities*
3 *Communication. This refers to a student's general ability to express ideas and opinions, with confidence and clarity, to a variety of audiences for a variety of purposes*
4 *Teamwork. This refers to a student's general ability to work productively in different kinds of team (formal, informal, project based, committee based etc)*
5 *Problem solving. This refers to a student's general ability to identify the main features of a given problem and to develop strategies for its resolution.*

A 1997 University of Nottingham small scale study (Murphy et al 1997) looked at 200 students from various disciplines from 10 universities, assessing their competence at level 3 of the QCA key skills specifications (for Communication, Application of Number, IT, Improving own Learning and Performance, Working with Others). The students were assessed, were asked to self assess, and tutors in the schools and colleges from which they had come were also asked to gauge the students' competence. The report is cautious and emphasises that its findings are indicative only (there were difficulties, for example the sample was small and for practical reasons composed of volunteers, there were more women than men, there were relatively few mature students and the entry qualifications tended to be A level, there are limited assessment tools available). The main findings were:

- 66% were at or above level 3 in Communication, 44% in Application of Number, 47% in IT, 41% in Improving own Learning and Performance and 62% in Working with Others
- 18% were at level 3 or above in all three skills of Communication, Application of Number and IT, 16% did not meet level 3 in any of them, and 6% were at level 3 or above in all 5 key skills
- male students were more competent in Application of Number and IT, female students more competent in Communication, and there were no significant gender differences for the other key skills
- more students in 'established' universities met the competence thresholds than those from new universities, apart from in IT, the largest difference being in Application of Number
- there was a strong link between A level performance and key skill competence
- arts students performed worse than broad science students in Communication and Application of Number, but the differences in IT were small
- students and tutors estimates of the competence levels did not always agree with the assessments. This may both point to the inadequacy of current assessment methods available and may also indicate that students find it difficult to evaluate their own performance (a crucial aspect of Improving own Learning and Performance).

The report considers possible policy implications from its findings: assessing key skills is expensive and would require considerable resources; given the low proportion of students with level 3 in all key skills requiring this level at entry in the near future would adversely affect intake numbers; institutions wishing to bring all their first year students to level 3 will face a considerable challenge; universities ignoring key skill deficiencies are likely to face considerable barriers to learning and progress; a debate is needed about whether key skills should improve through HE (at the moment there is little information about whether or not they do, but NCIHE's 1997 report implies that they should improve through HE).

The university sector as a whole does seem to face a considerable challenge in moving towards the recommendations in Dearing's report on HE, in the light of the report by Muphy et al. This perception is reinforced by the findings of the LTI's own internal survey, which suggested little agreement amongst universities about the frameworks to be used and that very few are using the QCA key skill descriptors which Dearing refers to. Murphy's respondents were mainly young people who entered HE at age 18 and who can be expected to have experienced at least some of the initiatives outlined above, yet their key skill level appeared to be low. This may reflect reality, or it may reflect shortcomings in our ability to assess skills.

4 Summary

This paper has outlined the main political and economic justifications for skills approaches: the individual has a crucial role in creating a successful economy; change is rapid and individuals must adapt and transfer their skills and learning to new situations; education is very expensive and must justify itself, to a large extent, in terms of the development of individuals who can contribute to the economy. The paper has also critically reviewed the assumptions behind these views. Whether or not the views are capable of substantiation, they have made an enormous impact on education in general and HE in particular and are virtually unchallenged.

These views have led to a series of initiatives designed to encouraged the development of 'transferable skills' in students, most notably during the 1980s and 1990s. These initiatives have been at every level of education and training, at school, in FE, at the workplace, and in HE.

In spite of this focus and the investment in it, for example via TVEI, EHE, NCVQ, there are unanswered questions which emerge in the course of this review of the history of the skills movement. Are 'transferable skills' transferable? What transfers and how can that transfer be aided? Have skills approaches in education actually improved skill levels (and if not, is this because 'transfer' has not taken place)? Does a focus on skills improve performance in education or at work? In what way do individual skills impact upon the success of an organisation? Is there a need for a nationally understood definition of skills, or should institutions develop their own, relevant to their contexts? How can skill levels be assessed, what exactly is being assessed (in group work, for example) and how important is this in an 'accountable' society? Given the investment in this area, these seem to be worthwhile questions to address.

Sue Drew, LTI Sheffield Hallam University
20.10.97

References

Key skills in Higher Education: background and rationale.

AGR (1995) *Skills for Graduates in the 21st Century.* Cambridge, Association of Graduate Recruiters.

Anderson A, Marshall V (1996) *Core versus occupation specific skills. Research Studies RS12.* DFEE HMSO

Ashworth J (1985) "Tomorrow's Universities: Ivory Towers, Frontier Posts or Service Stations" from *Educating for Tomorrow: the 1985 Cantor Lectures*, RSA.

Atkins M (1995) "What should we be assessing" in Knight P (Ed) *Assessment for Learning in HE* Kogan Page.

Baker K (1989) Sec of State speech to ACFHE February 1989. Published as: *Further Education: a new strategy. Department of Education and Science*

Barnett C (1986) *The Audit of War*, MacMillan.

Beurett G & Webb A (1983) *The Goals of Engineering Education. Project conducted by Leicester Polytechnic*, CNNA Development Services Publication.

Binks M "Enterprise in Higher Education and the Graduate Labour Market". *Education and Training* Vol 38 No 2 1996 p26-29

Boys, Brennan et al. (1988) *Higher Education and the Preparation for Work,* Jessica Kingsley.

BTEC (1984) *Policies and Priorities into the 1990s,* BTEC

Burgess T (1977) *Education after School,* Victor Gollancz.

Burgess T & Pratt J (1974) *Polytechnics: A Report,* Pitman Publishing.

Callaghan J (22 Oct 1976) "Towards a National Debate" (The Ruskin Speech) *Education,* (Journal of the Association of Education Committees), Volume 148 No 17 pp 332-333.

CBI (1990) *"Towards a Skills Revolution"* CBI

Central Policies Review Staff (1980) *Education, Training and Industrial Performance;* HMSO.

Chambers J (1986) *Personal Effectiveness,* Occasional Paper No 13. RSA

CNAA (1989) *Handbook 1989,* CNAA

Committee on Manpower Resources for Science and Technology, (Chairman - Prof M Swann (1968) *The Flow into Employment of Scientists, Engineers and Technologists*, HMSO.

Confederation of British Industry (1989) *Towards a Skills Revolution.* CBI.

Council for Industry and Higher Education (1987) *Towards a Partnership. Higher Education-Government-Industry.*

CSU (1990) *Graduate Employment Prospects 1990,* CSU.

CSU (1992) *Statistical Quarterly Vacancy Survey June 1992).* CSU.

Dale R (Ed) (1985) *Education, Training and Employment: Towards a New Vocationalism,* Pergammon Press.

Dearing R (1997) *Review of Qualifications for 16-19 year olds. Full Report.* SCAA.

Department for Education and Welsh Office (1992) *Choice and diversity: a new framework for schools* (Cmd 2021) HMSO.

Department of Education and Science (1985) *Better Schools,* (Cmd 9469) HMSO.

Department of Education and Science (1991) *Higher Education: a new Framework,* HMSO Cm 1541).

Department of Education and Science (1987) *Higher Education - Meeting the Challenge,* White Paper (Cmnd 114) HMSO.

Department of Education and Science (May 1995) *The Development of Higher Education into the 1990s,* (Cmd 9524) HMSO.

Department of Employment (Dec 1988) *Employment for the 1990s, White Paper,* HMSO.

Department of Employment and Education and Science (July 1986) *Working Together Education and Training*, (Cmd 114) HMSO.

Department of Trade and Industry, (1994) *Competitiveness: helping business win,* (Cm 2563) HMSO.

Department of Trade and Industry (1995) *Competitiveness: forging ahead,* (Cm 2867), HMSO.

(1988) *Education Reform Act,* Elizabeth II. Chapter 40 HMSO.

Education, Science and Arts Committee (1980) *The Funding and Organisation of Courses in Higher Education 5th Report from the Education, Science and Arts Committee of the House of Commons 1979-80,* (HC 787-1) HMSO.

Employment Department (1991) *The First Year of Enterprise in Higher Education* Employment Department.

Employment Department, Scottish Office and Welsh Office (1992) *People, jobs and opportunity,* (Cm 1810) HMSO.

Faure (1972) *Learning to be. The World of Today and Tomorrow. Report of the International Committee on the development of Education,* UNESCO Paris.

FEU (May 1989) *Extending TVEI,* Bulletin 1. FEU.

Finniston Sir M (Chairman) (1980) *Engineering our Future. report of the Committee of Enquiry into the Engineering Profession*, HMSO Cmnd 7794.

Foucault M (1977) *Discipline and Punish.* Penguin.

Gordon A (1983) Attitudes of Employers to the recruitment of graduates *Educational Studies,* Vol 9 No 3.

Handy C (1984) *Organising for Capability,* Occasional Paper No 4. RSA.

Handy C, Gordon C, et al (1988) *Making Managers,* Pitman.

Handy C, Gow I, et al (1987) *The Making of Managers. A Report on Management Education Training and Development in the USA, West Germany, France, Japan and the UK*, MSC, NEDO, BIM.

Harvey L, Moon S, Geall V with Bower R (1997) *Graduates' Work: organisational change and students' attributes.* Birmingham, Centre for Research into Quality, University of Central England at Birmingham.

HEQC (1995) *Graduate Standards Programme. Interim Report Executive Summary* HERQC.

HEQC Quality Enhancement Group (1996) *A paper to stimulate discussion. What are graduates? (Clarifying the attributes of "graduateness"* HEQC.

Higginson G (Chairman) (1988) *Advancing A Levels,* DES and Welsh Office HMSO.

Hirch W and Bevan S (1988) *What makes a Manager,* Institute of Manpower Studies, Brighton: University of Sussex.

Hudson G (1996) Dealing with Work: secondary students' work experience and the curriculum in *Journal of Vocational Education and Training Vol 48, No 3, pp177-294*

Jenkins A (March 1997). *Transferable skills at Oxford Brookes University . Policy in Summary.* Oxford, Oxford Centre for Staff and Learning Development.

Joint Board for Pre-Vocational Education (May 1984) *The Certificate of Pre-Vocational Education Consultative Document,* Joint Board of Pre-Vocational Education.

Joint Board for Pre-Vocational Education (1989) *CPVE and National Vocational Qualifications*, Joint Board of Pre-Vocational Education.

Jones A (1985) "Tommorrow's Schools"; closed or open, from *Educating for Tomorrow: The 1985 Cantor Lectures*, RSA.

Levy M (1987) *The Core Skills Project and work Based Learning,* MSC.

Levy M and Matthews D (March 1989) *The MSC Core Skills,* The Further Education Staff college Information Bank Work-Based Learning Paper. FESC.

Matthews D (1986) *The accreditation of ability to transfer skills and knowledge to new situations.* A paper for discussion by the Youth Certification Board. FESC

McGeevor P and Brennan J (1990) *Ethnic Minorities and the Graduate Labour Market,* Commission for racial Equality.

Morning J (1988) *CPVE Evaluation. General Findings and Recommendations,* BTEC and CGLI.

MSC (May 1977) *Young People at Work. Report on the Feasibility of a New Programme of Opportunities for Unemployed Young People, MSC.*

MSC (1981) A New Training Initiative. A Consultative Document, MSC.

MSC/NEDO (1984) *Competence and Competition - Training and Education in the Federal Republic of Germany, The United States and Japan. A Report prepared by the Institute of Manpower Studies for the National Economic Development Council and the MSC,* NEDO.

Murphy R; Burke P; Gillespie J; Rainbow R; Wilmut J (1997) *The Key Skills of Students Entering Higher Education.* Nottingham University of Nottingham School of Education.

NAB (May 1986) *Transferable Skills in Employment - The Contribution of Higher Education.*

National Curriculum Council (March 1990). *Core Skills 16-19. Response to the Secretary of State.* NCC.

NCIHE (National Committee of Inquiry into HE) (Chairman R Dearing) (1997) *Higher Education in the Learning Society. Summary Report.* London, NCIHE.

NCVQ (Oct 1989) *The Extension of the NVQ Framework above level IV. A Consultative Document,* NCVQ.

NCVQ (June 1995) *GNVQ Briefing. Information on the form, development and implementation of GNVQs.* NCVQ

NCVQ (1996) *Core Skills* London, NCVQ.

Neath M *The Development and Transfer of Undergraduate Group Work Skills* (uncompleted doctoral thesis, Sheffield Hallam University, 1997)

Newman J H (1853) *The idea of a University.* Oxford University Press

Oates T (1992) Core skills and transfer: Aiming high. *Educational and Training Technology International Vol 29 No.3 pp 227-39*

Oates T (1992) *Report 16 Developing and piloting the NCVQ Core Skills. An outline of method and a summary of findings* NCVQ

Otter S (1992) *Learning Outcomes in Higher Education.* UDACE/FEU.

PCFC (March 1989) *Funding Choices. Methods of Funding Higher Education in Polytechnics and colleges. A Consultative Document,* The Polytechnics and Colleges Funding Council.

Pratt J and Silverman S (1988) *Responding to Constraint. Policy and Management in Higher Education,* SRHE and Open University Press.

Robbins Lord (Chairman) (1963) *Higher Education: Report of the Committee appointed by the Prime Minister,* HMSO.

Roizen J and Jepson M (1985) *Degrees for Jobs,* SRHE and NFER-Nelson.

RSA (1980) *Education for Capability,* RSA.

RSA (1997) *Key Skills. Information Brief.* RSA

SCOEG (1985) *Response of the Standing Conference of Employers of Graduates (SCOEG) to the Green Paper on the Development of Higher Education into the 1990s,* SCOEG.

Scottish Office (1991) *Access and opportunity: a strategy for education and training. (Cm 1530) HMSO*

Sheffield TEC. (1997) *Sheffield Training & Enterprise Council Annual Report 1995-1996* Sheffield TEC.

Singley M K and Anderson J R (1989) *The transfer of cognitive skill.* Havard University Press

Smith D and Blackham R D (1988) The measurement of managerial abilities in an assessment centre. *Personnel Review,* 17(4) pp 15-21.

Smith D, Wolstencroft T and Southern J (1989) *Personal Transferable Skills and the Job Demands on Graduates,* Huddersfield Polytechnic.

Spens W Chairman) (1938) *Report of the consultative Committee on Secondary Education with Special Reference to Grammar Schools and Technical High Schools,* HMSO.

Stephenson J (1988) *Facing the Challenge of Higher Education for Capability,* RSA.

Thames Valley University (May 1997) *Using the SEEC Descriptors.* London. Thames Valley University.

Trades Union Congress (1989) *Skills 2000.* TUC

Training Agency (March 1988) *Development of Assessable Standards for National Certification.*

   Guidance Note 1. A Code of Practice and a Development Model, 1988

   Guidance Note 2. Developing standards by Reference to functions, 1989.

   Guidance Note 3. The definition of Competences and Performance Criteria, March 1988.

   Guidance Note 4. The Characteristics of Units of Competence, March 1988.

   Guidance Note 5. Assessment of Competence, Jan 1889.

   Guidance Note 6. Verification or Monitoring of Assessment Practice, Jan 1889.

Training Agency (1989) *Enterprise in Training Information Pack,* Training Agency.

Training Agency (1990) *Enterprise in Higher Education. Key Features of the Enterprise in Higher Education Proposals 1889-90,* Training Agency.

Training Agency (1990) *The current role of TVEI. Focus Statement.* Training Agency.

Waddell Sir J (Chairman) July 1978) *School Examinations. report of the Steering Committee established to consider replacing the GCE O Level and the CSE by a common system of examining, Part 1,* HMSO Cmnd 7281-1.

Walker   L (Ed) (1995) *Institutional Change. Towards an Ability-Based Curriculum in Higher Education. Conference Report.* Sheffield, Employment Department

Waugh C (Autumn 1988) *"Polytechnical Education and Vocational Preparation" Liberal Education and General Education,* Journal of the Natfhe General Studies Section, p 28-36, Issue 61.

Williams Prof G (1985) *"Graduate Employment and Vocationalism in Higher Education",* European Journal of Education, Vol 20 Nos 2-3, p 181-192.